The Art of Miracles

UNLOCK YOUR PSYCHIC GIFTS TO TRANSFORM YOUR LIFE

YAMUNA & AYESHA HASAN

CREATIVE CORP
MEDIA

CREATIVE CORP MEDIA

Dedication

Your soul has been looking for this knowledge for an eternity, and we have waited for you until the beginning of time. This moment has been divinely orchestrated so you can live the life of miracles you were born to live. This book was written for you.

Contents

Introduction   IX

1. The Foundation   1

2. The History   7

3. Your Gifts   19

4. Meditation   33

5. How to Meditate   41

6. What is the Divine?   57

7. Enlightenment   67

Epilogue   93

References   99

Contact   103

Introduction

WHAT IS YOUR SOUL LOOKING FOR?

What is your soul looking for?

This is the question that can drive you *crazy*, haunt your existence, and keep you up at night. It is the question you cannot get out of your head no matter how hard you try or do, and it remains unanswered.

The question that burns in your soul as you desperately search for an answer. What are you looking for?

You've yearned for years for the answer. It may feel like you've tried *everything* to get that answer. It may have felt like all your hope has been lost, and you're just meant to exist. Not live, but exist. Because you don't know what you're looking for. You don't know what that is, but you know it's for you, and you know it's something bigger than you could ever imagine. It feels like an eternity of endlessly searching for that *bigger* thing.

You're lost in an infinite maze, like a puzzle in which all the pieces don't fit – the never-ending search - the empty fire left to burn and lost and in the dark, trying to find answers, the light. You were led astray on a path that leads to nowhere. What are you searching for? Something comes to your mind. You don't have words for it yet, but you know what we're discussing. The answer to that question may feel *impossible* to find. But it's been in front of you this whole time. Right under your nose, the very thing you've been looking for. What you've been searching for. What keeps you up at night? It's right in front of you. It's *in* you. It *is* you. The answer to that eternal question... is in the essence of your being, your soul.

That *burning desire* in your soul. That never-ending feeling screams at you that you are meant for something bigger. Something *extraordinary*, something so big you cannot put it into words. That feeling that you're not meant to live and die in the ordinary. That feeling you get when you know you are here for something so *grand* you cannot put it into words. How long will you leave that call unanswered? How long *can* you? Before the screaming becomes so loud you can't hear anything else - that *burning desire* - with the flame becoming stronger every moment until the "ordinary" is burnt down. What is no longer meant for you will fall apart. That job, that person, that situation all comes crashing down. When the flames of your burning desire become so strong, when the screaming blurs out every other noise, when your soul *calls*, you must answer.

You may ignore that call.

Many do, and that's why they stay stuck in a never-ending cycle of "I'm meant for something bigger, but I don't know what it is." However, when that call goes unanswered, so does the life of miracles you were born to live. Imagine how many times you have declined that call. How often have you neglected that strong, magnificent desire in your soul? The calling that you are meant for is *so much more*.

Because you are!

Your soul has been looking for your psychic gifts this whole time. We know this sounds shocking, but it is the very truth that is written onto your soul. It is the same reason that you were *called* to read this book. Deep down, your soul has been leading you home, right back to the answer to your search. Ultimately, everything you do is a search for your psychic gifts. This is why it feels like something's missing; you've been searching your whole life to fill it. Here's the appalling thing: You can reach the highest levels of success, complete all your goals, and be where you dreamed of but still have an absence. An absence of *something*. An absence that demands to be known, but you still do not know what. This absence is the lack of your psychic gifts in *your* life, and the only way to fill them is to unlock them.

How do you do that?

To step into your psychic gifts.

Why are your psychic gifts so important?

Your psychic gifts are...

- The *answer* to all of your problems.

- The precious guide that will guide you to all of your miracles.

- Your ultimate protection against danger.

- Works as a conductor, orchestrating the right people, places, situations, and events for you.

- Expands your health boundlessly into perfection.

- Transforms your relationships with a sense of clarity and higher knowledge.

- Triples your abundance to astounding levels, in your business and financially, by knowing what divine strategies to implement to increase your wealth and so much more.

How do we know this?

Meet your guides

One day, deep in meditation, a thundering voice boomed and said,

"Write"

The most beautiful light surrounded us. It was blinding to the eyes but touching to the soul. As we looked around in shock, trying to comprehend what had just happened, it continued to immerse us in its ablaze glow. It was the divine, with a message for us.

> *"You need to write a book. This book will enlighten my creation with the wonders of learning how to meditate and teach the profound benefits of stepping into your psychic gifts and intuition."*

At this very moment, we didn't know that this message would transform our lives *forever*.

We are Yamuna and Ayesha, the living embodiment of Divine truth and Divine power. Together, we are a dynamic duo dedicated to helping you embrace the miraculous life you were destined for. With years of experience as spiritual healers, we have empowered many to lead lives filled with miracles. As global entrepreneurs, our clientele spans the globe. We are on a mission to share these gifts with everyone, to change the world, and to start the golden age.

On our journey, by learning how to meditate and stepping into *our* psychic gifts and intuition, our lives drastically changed. Because of this gift, so many miracles have happened. Relocating from Beverly Hills to Dubai, starting the business of our dreams, and transforming the lives of our clients, we honestly cannot tell you *how impactful* your psychic gifts are. All of this is possible with your psychic gifts. After a three-year-long journey of researching this ancient and timeless truth, countless revisions, and fascinating discoveries, this book is finally done. This was written by the Divine *for you* to unlock your life's ultimate change. So you can receive boundless abundance, rejoice in your relationships, and experience radiant health.

By stepping into our psychic gifts, we have drastically transformed our lives and the lives of our clients.

"I've been working with Yamuna and Ayesha remotely for the last two years, and I can't believe the rapid changes that have occurred for myself and my business. I had reached a point where I was stuck, overwhelmed by my pain and grief from losing loved ones. Consequently, my business started going downhill, and I wasn't experiencing any growth. However, Yamuna and Ayesha's guidance and input guided me to step into my psychic gifts, and seeing and hearing God brought me to tears and helped me get out of my way and heal so many aspects of myself. I am now making six figures and am in a healthy place both mentally and physically. I continue to work with them and check in on myself. The great thing about working with Yamuna and Ayesha is that their coaching has helped me and benefited my entire team. I now pay for my employees to check in and work with them every week, ensuring that my whole company continues to flourish."

Angel R.

"Working with Yamuna and Ayesha has completely transformed my love life. Before meeting them, I was carrying a heavy burden of pain from past relationships, which made it difficult for me to open my heart to love fully. I felt disconnected and unsure of how to build the deep, meaningful relationship I longed for. Yamuna and Ayesha's help has been nothing short of miraculous. They helped me look within and heal the wounds holding me back. With their support, I learned to embrace vulnerability and trust in love again. They showed me how to see the divine in my relationship, bringing a new level of depth and connection I never thought possible. I'm in a loving, fulfilling relationship where I feel truly seen and cherished. I can give and receive love with an open heart, and I'm so grateful to Yamuna and Ayesha for guiding me on this journey. They have helped me find the love and connection I was searching for, and for that, I am eternally thankful."

William T.

"My journey with Yamuna and Ayesha has been transformative for my health. I was struggling with chronic IBS, sleepless nights, and an overwhelming sense of fatigue that made it hard to get through each day. I felt trapped in a cycle of discomfort and exhaustion, relying on medication to manage my symptoms.

Yamuna and Ayesha helped me get to the core of my issues in a way I never thought possible. I began understanding the deeper connections between my mind, body, and spirit. They provided me with the tools and insights to address the root causes of my health challenges rather than just treating the symptoms.

As I worked with them, I slowly started to see improvements. My sleep began to normalize, my energy levels increased, and my IBS symptoms became more manageable. With their support, I was able to gradually wean off my medication, something I never imagined I could do.

Today, I feel more in tune with my body and more empowered in my health than ever. They have been a guiding light on my path to wellness, and I am deeply grateful for their help in reclaiming my health and vitality."

Charlotte S.

Imagine the change and transformation stepping into *your* psychic gifts can do for you...How different would your life be than it is today? Imagine the clarity in your relationships, financial abundance, and the vitality you can experience in your health. It's time to make this a reality, and *you can* do so by unleashing your psychic gifts and expanding the magnificent power of your intuition.

Are you ready? Let's begin your transcendent awakening!

CHAPTER ONE

The Foundation

According to quantum physics, at the fundamental level, everything in the universe, including matter and particles, is made up of energy. Quantum physics explores the behavior of particles on a microscopic scale and has shown us that matter can exist in multiple states simultaneously, known as superposition. This suggests that particles, at their core, are not solid entities but rather energy waves. Additionally, the famous equation $E=mc^2$, proposed by Albert Einstein, demonstrates the equivalence of energy and matter. It shows that energy and mass are interchangeable; in simple terms, everything is energy. $E=mc^2$ is Einstein's famous equation and is a groundbreaking formula that shows the relationship between energy (E), mass (m), and the speed of light (c). In simple terms, it demonstrates that mass and energy are interchangeable. When an object has mass, it also contains tremendous potential energy. The equation reveals that a small mass can be converted into a large amount of energy and vice versa. This concept is crucial in understanding that everything in the universe, including matter, is essentially a form of energy. The equation implies that even the most solid-seeming objects are made up of energy at their core.

Quantum physics also introduces entanglement, where particles can become linked regardless of the distance between them, implying a profound connection to energy within the fabric of reality. These captivating discoveries in quantum physics provide a scientific basis for understanding that everything, from the tiniest subatomic particles to the vast expanse of the universe, is interconnected and composed of energy.

However, this revolutionary discovery didn't just change the world of physics forever, but the world itself. The equation played a crucial role in the development of nuclear weapons and power, shaping the course of history. Furthermore, $E=mc^2$ laid the foundation for a myriad of scientific advancements, including nuclear fission and fusion research, particle physics, and even space exploration. Its influence extends far beyond the realm of physics, impacting technology, medicine, and our overall understanding of existence.

This astonishing discovery also had a profound psychological impact. This revolutionary formula challenged traditional views of matter, energy, and the nature of existence. It introduced the concept that everything, including ourselves, is fundamentally composed of energy, causing shock and wonder across the world and a feeling of how deeply intertwined we are with the Divine. The equation's implications transcend scientific boundaries and delve into existential questions about the nature of reality, consciousness, and the universe's mysterious workings.

This revolution isn't only found in Einstein's equation but throughout history across the globe. Every place, everywhere, far and near, there has been an inexplicable connection between humanity and the divine. This connection has always existed and can be found from ancient times to today's modern world. Quantum physics is modern proof of what has been known for thousands of years, so let's take a deeper look at this ancient and timeless truth.

CHAPTER TWO

The History

Ancient China

Chi, also known as Qi, is an essential concept in traditional Chinese culture and medicine. It is the vital life force or energy that flows through all living things. The history of Chi can be traced back thousands of years in ancient China.

In Chinese philosophy, Chi is the fundamental building block of the universe, connecting all existence. When Chi is balanced, it is harmonious for the body and improves health and well-being. Tai chi and Qigong are practices aimed at elevating and balancing Chi through control of your breath, movement, and meditation. These techniques promote physical, mental, and spiritual harmony. These practices have been passed down from generation to generation and are extensively practiced today.

The history of Chi is deeply rooted in the ancient and profound wisdom of Chinese culture and continues to be an influential aspect of holistic health and spiritual practices.

This concept has widely influenced various aspects of Chinese culture, including feng shui, acupuncture, and martial arts. The understanding of Chi has changed the world by promoting a holistic approach to health and well-being that focuses on balancing energy flow within the body. It has also influenced Western medicine and alternative healing modalities, leading to a greater appreciation of the mind-body connection and the role of energy in health.

Ancient India

Prana is a concept entrenched in ancient Indian spirituality and philosophy. Prana is the vital life force or energy that permeates all living beings and the entire universe. It is known as the essence of life itself, sustaining and spiriting everything. The history of prana can be traced back thousands of years in the Indian subcontinent, where it has been a central concept in many spiritual practices and disciplines. In yoga, pranayama is the practice of harnessing the breath to activate and balance prana in the body. In the traditional Indian system of medicine, Ayurveda also recognizes the significance of prana in sustaining mental and physical well-being. Prana is said to extend beyond the individual body and is a connector to the more considerable cosmic energy.

This has had an unfathomable impact on the world. Understanding prana has influenced many aspects of life, including meditation and traditional healing practices.

The concept of prana has changed the world by introducing a holistic approach to health and overall well-being, emphasizing the fascinating link of the mind, body, and spirit. It has inspired people worldwide to explore alternative forms of medicine, energy healing, and mindfulness practices that focus on harmonizing the flow of prana within the body. The concept of prana has also influenced modern psychology and wellness approaches, encouraging a more comprehensive understanding of health that incorporates physical, mental, emotional, and spiritual aspects.

Ancient Egypt

Ancient Egypt holds a rich opulence of spirituality that has altered society and culture. From Cleopatra to the pyramids, the ancient spirituality of Egypt has mesmerized many. Their spirituality was intensely intertwined with their lives, rituals, and beliefs about the soul's journey beyond the physical passing, also known as death. The concept of Ma'at, representing balance, order, and truth, was essential to Egyptian spirituality, guiding both personal conduct and cosmic harmony. The intricate rituals, symbols, and beliefs of ancient Egyptian spirituality reflected a profound reverence for the cycles of life, death, and rebirth, shaping their worldview and leaving a lasting legacy that has transcended time.

Not only is this connection found in places, but also in people. Throughout time, era after era, individuals with psychic abilities have captured the attention of people across the globe. The concept of psychics can be traced back to ancient times when seers, oracles, and diviners were revered for their ability to tap into the spiritual realm and access information beyond the physical world. From years of prosperous knowledge to today's modern world, Let's delve into the intriguing history of psychics.

The Oracle Of Delphi

The Oracle of Delphi was a revered priestess who served as a communicator between the physical world and the spiritual realm. Present in the sanctuary of Apollo at Delphi, Greece, she was considered the most prestigious and prominent oracle in ancient times. People from all over, including kings, politicians, and ordinary individuals, would travel great distances to seek her insight and guidance. The prophecies of the Oracle of Delphi shaped essential decisions, such as politics, matters of war, and personal choices. The oracle's reputation for accuracy and divine connection made her a crucial figure in the ancient world. The sanctuary of Delphi became a place for spiritual journeys, attracting visitors from far and wide.

Edgar Cayce

Edgar Cayce was born in Kentucky, USA, in 1877. He discovered his psychic abilities early in his lifetime, but it wasn't until he entered a meditative trance-like state that his abilities truly awakened. During this state, Cayce would provide in-depth readings on various topics, including spirituality, health, past lives, and future events. He became acclaimed for his ability to provide accurate diagnoses of illnesses and offered holistic treatments, often called "Cayce remedies." People from near and far yearned for his healing and guidance. Cayce's remedies were documented, forming the foundation of the Association for Research and Enlightenment (ARE) to preserve and study his work. His contributions to the field of psychic phenomena have left a lasting impact, and his teachings continue to inspire and intrigue people worldwide.

Ingo Swann

Ingo Swann was a highly gifted and influential figure in the field of remote viewing. He played a significant role in the Stargate Project, exhibiting his extraordinary psychic abilities. One of his many notable successes was when he was given a sealed envelope containing a coordinate, and without any prior knowledge, he accurately described intricate details of the location, including specific features, structures, and details. This electrifying demonstration of his remote viewing abilities astounded researchers and added to the practical applications of psychic phenomena.

Ingo Swann's contributions extended beyond the Stargate Project. He has written several books on remote viewing and consciousness exploration, sharing his insights and experiences with the world. His work helped popularize the concept of remote viewing and sparked interest in the broader field of parapsychology.

Ingo Swann's legacy continues to captivate those interested in psychic phenomena and the exploration of human consciousness. His remarkable abilities and contributions to the Stargate Project and beyond have left an indelible mark on the world of parapsychology.

John Edward

John Edward, a prominent psychic medium, has left a significant mark on the world of psychic phenomena and spiritual guidance. Edward came to fame through his television show "Crossing Over with John Edward," showcasing his ability to communicate with spirits from the other side. His compassionate and empathetic approach to delivering messages from departed loved ones connected with audiences worldwide, earning him a loyal following. Edward's work as a medium has helped countless individuals find comfort, closure, and peace by connecting them with messages from the spirit world. Through his live events, books, and media appearances, Edward continues to impact the lives of many, being a doorway between the physical and spiritual realms with his unique gift.

These extraordinary gifts exist in you and are waiting to be unleashed. These people are not unlike you and are not part of some chosen few with extraordinary abilities you do not have. Everyone is born with their sixth sense, but these gifts can get shut down over time in society. Instead of embracing this gift and, as a result, reaping the rich rewards it, we've been taught quite the opposite...It's time for you to unleash these gifts and reap their rich rewards.

Are you ready to learn *how* to step into your psychic gifts?

CHAPTER THREE

Your Gifts

Your psychic gifts have always been there and must be developed. Like your five senses, your intuition is a sense that needs to be developed. To do this very easily, you need to develop your gift! Your psychic gifts are like beautiful flowers yet to bloom into greatness. You have to nurture, practice, and develop your gifts for them to bloom wondrously. Your principal psychic gifts are clairvoyance (seeing), clairaudience (hearing), clairsentience (feeling), claircognizance (knowing), and clairempathy (emotion). Although essential but lesser known are clairgustance (taste), clairalience (smell), and clairtangency (touch). Blended, the result is marvelous.

Clairvoyance

Clairvoyance is a psychic ability that involves you perceiving information about a person, object, location, or physical event through extrasensory perception. People with clairvoyance have the gift of seeing things beyond the physical world. Having clairvoyance can allow you to predict the future, see auras, or perceive spiritual beings. Clairvoyants may receive visions, symbols, or mental images that provide insights into past, present, and future events. It's like having a sixth sense that allows you to tap into information that is not readily available through the typical five senses. Many cultures and belief systems have different interpretations of clairvoyance, but at its core, it involves accessing knowledge or insights beyond what can be explained by science or logic.

Clairaudience

Clairaudience is a psychic ability that involves receiving information through hearing things beyond the ordinary auditory senses. People with clairaudient abilities may hear voices, sounds, or messages from the spirit world or higher realms. It's like having an inner ear that can tune into messages not audible to others. This phenomenon is often linked to spiritual communication, where individuals may receive guidance, warnings, or insights through these auditory experiences.

Clairsentience

Clairsentience is a psychic ability that allows you to sense information and emotions beyond what your regular senses can detect. It's like having a superpower where you can feel things others can't. People with clairsentient abilities might pick up on vibes, energies, or emotions from places, objects, or other people. It's as if they have an intuitive radar that helps them understand the unseen aspects of a situation. Clairsentience is often linked with empathy and heightened sensitivity to the feelings and energies around them. In essence, clairsentience is like having a special gift to sense and interpret subtle energies and emotions that lie beneath the surface of our everyday experiences.

Claircognizance

Claircognizance is a psychic ability where you know things without any logical or prior explanation. It's like having a deep inner knowing or intuition that provides insights or information without any apparent source. People with claircognizant abilities might suddenly understand a situation, have ideas pop into their heads, or receive knowledge about something without explaining how they got that information. It's as if they have a direct line to the universal knowledge database. In essence, claircognizance is like having a built-in information superhighway that gives you access to knowledge beyond what can be explained by ordinary means.

Clairempathy

Clairempathy is a psychic ability where you can feel or experience the emotions and energies of others as if they were your own. It's like having an empathic connection that transcends normal boundaries, allowing people to sense and understand the feelings and moods of those around them on a deep emotional level. Those with clairempathic abilities may suddenly experience intense emotions that are not their own, picking up on the emotional states of others and having insight into their inner worlds. It's as if they are tuning into the emotional frequencies of the people they encounter, creating a profound sense of understanding and empathy.

Clairtangency

Clairtangency, also known as psychometry, is a psychic ability where you can perceive information about an object or person by touching it. It's like having a heightened sense of touch that allows people to pick up on the energy and history associated with an object through physical contact. Those with clairtangent abilities may receive impressions, images, emotions, or insights when holding an object, providing them with a glimpse into the past or the essence of the object's owner. It's as if they can tap into the energetic residue left on objects and interpret the vibrations they sense.

In essence, clairtangency offers a unique way for individuals to access hidden knowledge and insights by interacting with the physical world. It expands our understanding of perception and the unseen energies that surround us.

Clairgustance

Clairgustance is a psychic ability that allows one to receive information through taste. People with clairgustant abilities may suddenly perceive specific tastes or flavors associated with a person, place, or situation, providing them with messages or intuitive insights. It's as if they are experiencing a gustatory sensation on a spiritual or energetic level. In essence, clairgustance offers a unique way of receiving information through the sense of taste.

Clairalience

Clairalience is a psychic ability that gives you a heightened sense of smell beyond the ordinary, allowing people to perceive scents or odors associated with spirits, energies, or past events. Those with clairalience abilities may suddenly detect specific fragrances or smells that hold symbolic or meaningful messages, providing them with warnings or intuitive insights. It's as if they are experiencing olfactory sensations on a spiritual or energetic level. In essence, clairalience offers a unique way of receiving information through the sense of smell, expanding our understanding of psychic phenomena and the vast capabilities of human perception beyond the physical realm.

With the use of these psychic gifts, massive transformation follows. The benefits of *using* your psychic gifts and following your intuition are illimitable, and let's look into some of them.

Truth and Clarity

Like a river flowing with crystal clear waters, immense clarity comes with your gift being open. Your life will flow beautifully, just like that river. Your miracles and blessings can flow easily when you know how to receive them, and You, your family, and your loved ones will be protected because you will know what to do and what not to do. Because it is not when the danger is upon us; it is *always* the moment before - when you got the warning and quickly got saved before the danger came. Your intuition will give you the right people, places, situations, and things because you will know who to talk to and who not to talk to. Who to be with and who not to be with. Who to deal with and who not to deal with. Your life then is crafted by perfection, magnificently by your gifts.

Your Questions, Finally, Answered.

Have you ever wondered what it would be like to have all your questions answered? You know, those questions that quietly seep into the back of your mind, searching for an answer. When your intuition constantly flows, your questions finally get their answers.

Problem? No, Solutions!

Whatever problems you are experiencing, your psychic gifts will give you solutions. When in darkness, your intuition is the light to guide you out of it. To help you reach the end of the tunnel that once seemed so far away.

CHAPTER FOUR

Meditation

The body is a magnificent instrument designed intricately by the divine, and its miraculous abilities continue to marvel the world. There has always been an incredible connection between the mind and body, With both constantly influencing the other in unthinkable ways. But how deep is this connection? Can the mind really influence the body? Can meditation improve your health? Well, these questions have answers, and let's take a look at them. Meditating is profoundly beneficial in *all* areas of your life. From astounding mental clarity and peace to scientifically proven physical benefits for your body, the benefits of meditating are endless.

Meditation lowers your blood pressure.

Many studies have been conducted to investigate the effects of meditation on blood pressure, and the results are quite fascinating. One study published in the journal Hypertension found that participants who practiced meditation experienced significant reductions in both systolic and diastolic blood pressure compared to a control group.

Another study conducted by researchers at the University of Kentucky found that mindfulness meditation can positively impact blood pressure. They found out that participants who engaged in an eight-week mindfulness-based stress reduction program experienced a significant decrease in systolic and diastolic blood pressure compared to a control group. In addition, a meta-analysis published in the journal Circulation: Cardiovascular Quality and Outcomes analyzed the combined results of multiple studies and found that meditation was associated with a substantial reduction in blood pressure.

Meditation reduces stress/lowers cortisol.

A profusion of studies have explored the effects of meditation on stress, and the results are intriguing. One study published in the Journal of Alternative and Complementary Medicine found that participants who practiced meditation experienced significant reductions in stress levels compared to individuals who did not participate in meditation.

Another study by researchers at Harvard Medical School found that meditation can change the brain's function and structure. Through neuroimaging techniques, they discovered that regular meditation practice can expand the thickness of the prefrontal cortex, which is responsible for functions such as emotional regulation and attention. This signifies that meditation helps us better cope with stress and make more mindful choices.

On top of that, research conducted at the University of California, Davis, found that meditation can modulate the activity of our genes. Specifically, they discovered that meditation can down-regulate the expression of genes associated with inflammation and stress response while up-regulating genes related to immune function and resilience.

Meditation benefits the immune system.

Several studies have shown that meditation can positively impact our immune system. One study published in Psychosomatic Medicine found that participants who experienced meditation had higher levels of antibodies, which play a crucial role in fighting off diseases and infections. Another study published in the journal Brain, Behavior, and Immunity discovered that meditation can increase the activity of natural killer cells, a type of white blood cell that helps recognize and eliminate harmful cells in the body, including cancer cells and viruses.

Meditation increases happiness.

Meditation is known to increase positivity and happiness, and many studies have proven this.

In one study, Compuware Corporation (a large business software and information technology services company) offered its employees group meditation sessions over a seven-week period. Participants were asked to practice meditation for at least 15-20 minutes per day, and the results were shocking. Results showed that this increased positive emotions and mindfulness and encouraged purpose. In addition, studies have shown that meditation can help combat depression. In the journal PubMed Central, studies have shown that meditation helps to disengage with negative thoughts and decrease depression-related thoughts and feelings and the chance of relapsing. Another study was published in PubMed Central, showing that meditation reduces anxiety. In this study, a six-week meditation program was implemented for university students. The results showed that anxiety and anxiety-related symptoms decreased. In a six-month and twelve-month follow-up, they found that the results were permanent for those who continued to meditate even after the program ended.

CHAPTER FIVE

How to Meditate

The most important way to develop your gifts is to *make* time to develop them. The world is constantly moving, buzzing, and, honestly, very loud. Making time to grow your gift in this noise can be challenging. But ask yourself, what can be louder than the call of your soul?

Pick a time in your day to sit down and develop your gift. This time shall be uninterrupted, where nothing will bother you or interfere. Whether it's in the morning when you first wake up or at night when it's quiet and no one's around. Pick a time that works best for *you*. This time is your reservation, your soul answering the calling it's yearned for. This time will be the foundation of receiving your miracles and will set your day for your soul's needed peace and tranquility. This moment is so unique and sacred. Every mighty oak was once a seed that took time to develop, grow, and flourish. You are yet to be a mighty oak, and your developed psychic gifts are the remarkable fruits you will bear! But first, grow your seed.

Let's discuss the most fundamental step to beginning your grand meditating journey: getting cleared. Many meditation techniques are transformative to your being, but getting cleared is the essential and most imperative technique.

Pro tip: For energy to flow best, sit in a lotus position while you meditate, with your legs crossed and spine straight.

Step One: still your mind

To truly harness the power of meditation, immerse yourself in a sacred space where you can fully surrender to the present moment. Close your eyes and let the outside world fade as you focus on your breath, feeling the energy flow through your body with each inhale and exhale. Dive deep within yourself, exploring the vast ocean of your consciousness, and embrace the stillness that resides within. Release all tension and resistance, letting peace wash over you like a gentle wave. Acknowledge them without attachment as thoughts arise, letting them drift away like clouds in the sky. Connect with the divine energy surrounding you, feeling a sense of oneness with all existence.

Step Two: see the light

Once you are relaxed, visualize a white light pouring into you—white, luminous, and blazing light. This is the Divine's light. Visualize this light pouring into your heart, mind, body, and soul in every single one of your trillions of cells, completely immersing you in it. An easy way to do this is to visualize the sun pouring into you.

Step Three: observe

As you're doing this, what comes up?

Pay attention to what you see. What colors do you see? If so, what colors are they? Are they darker or lighter? Do you see other people? If so, who are they? Why are they there?

Step Four: clearing

Tension, stress, negativity, chaos, pain, fear, anxiety, let it wash away with this light.

Clear all of this. Let the blinding white light pour into you and wash all of this away.

Tip: It's important to note not to clear any positive energies (such as bright colors, positive emotions like peace, joy, etc).

Now we've learned about the most fundamental step; it's time to discuss meditation techniques that are monumental to your being.

Bringing in abundance through meditation.

For best results, first get cleared. Once you are cleared, you are going to visualize blazing gold light. Pour that golden light into you and fully merge with this light. Merge your cells, organs, tissues, and whole body with this golden light. Then visualize a massive amount of abundance coming your way, and get *super specific* with this. You can visualize a heap of gold bars, specific money, or a new home. Then, step into the *feeling* of having it. How would you feel if you had that amount of money? How would you feel if you had gotten your new home? How would you feel if you had an abundance and overflow of money? Step into that feeling, whether it's joy, happiness, excitement, or purely emotion. Use all of your senses to tap into that feeling of having it. When you are done with this meditation, *embody* this feeling. Throughout the day, find ways to step into this feeling. Our clients have used this technique and *tripled* the amount of abundance in their lives - whether it's a new client that signed up for their program, made more money, or won on an investment, abundance flowed easily into their lives. You can repeat this as many times as you'd like.

Calling in your soul tribe through meditation.

If you are ready to meet the souls *destined* for you, this meditation is for you. The ones you were connected to long before you came into the physical realm, those that will help you grow exponentially, and those who get you. This is your soul tribe, or as we'd like to call it, your "Core Soul Group." To call in these people, first, you'd get cleared. Once you are done, visualize a rose-colored pink light. Pour this glowing and radiant pink light into you, encompassing your heart. Let your heart be bathed by this light, becoming clean of everything your heart is holding onto. Let it go, whether it's pain, resentment, sorrow, or betrayal, whatever is stored in your heart. Let this light reign in your heart, fully enveloping it. Once you can see that your heart is immersed in this light, you will repeat the following affirmation:

"I COMMAND THAT MY CORE SOUL GROUP COMES TO ME NOW."

You can experiment with these affirmations and see what works best for you, that makes you feel the most joy and the one you are comfortable with. And make sure to be specific, as you attract your "Core Soul Group", not anyone who will waste your time or lower your vibration. Our clients using this technique have reunited with lost loved ones, met their lifelong best friends, healed the relationship with some of their family members, and even met their soulmates. You can repeat this as much as you'd like.

Perfect health meditation.

This meditation focuses specifical.y on improving your health. Firstly, you will get cleared. After this, you will pour a bright blue and radiant green light into you. Pour this into your whole body: be very detailed. Truly flocd your body in this healing light. Once you are done, you will go very still and feel the inner state of your body. Hear your heartbeat. Quiet your mind. How does your body feel? An efficient way to do this is to visualize your body speaking to you. (Your heart, your brain, your stomach, etc.) what is your body saying? Is it saying to exercise more, to get more sunlight, to reduce your screen time, or to get moving? Is it sad, happy, or over-bounded with stress? *Hear* your body. Our clients who have used this technique have experienced remarkable results in their health, healing IBS, improving eyesight, and ridding chronic exhaustion. You can repeat this as much as you'd like.

Healing your inner child meditation.

This meditation technique is profoundly healing. You can start by visualizing your inner child.

What does your inner child look like? What are they wearing? What is the expression on their face? Are they happy or sad? Observe your inner child. Identify what it needs once you can fully and truly see your inner child. Does it need a giant hug to be reassured or told how loved it is? Understand what your inner child needs the most and give them that. This can look like:

- Giving your inner child a giant hug.

- Telling your inner child everything you love and admire about them.

- Telling your inner child everything you ever wished to hear when you were that age.

- Telling your inner child that everything will be alright, that they're safe to feel.

Get creative with your love, and shower your little you with tremendous affection.

You may cry during this meditation, but that's perfectly normal. After this, ask your inner child what you must do for complete healing. Do you need to play more, reconnect with your inner child more, or do something that little you would do? Spend as much time as you can with your inner child, and *do* what is asked of you for the final step. This meditation is so special because you're healing the most essential part of you to unite yourself truly.

Waterfalls of light meditation.

This meditation technique is one of our favorites and one of the most favored among our clients. Visualize a waterfall of light, with pearly white light that's sparkling, glistening, and glimmering, and gold light that's brilliant, glowing, and radiant. Use all of your senses to feel this light immensely. What does it smell like? What does it feel like? What is the texture of this glorious light pouring out of this waterfall? Once you can truly feel it, step into this waterfall. Let the light pour over you, and wash yourself clean. All your sorrows, stress, anxiety, pain, and fear are now being washed away in this glorious light. Anything negative on your mind, lay it down in this light. Let go of everything and immerse yourself in this experience. Stay there as long as you need, basking in this healing energy. Once you're done, you will feel so much more refreshed, energized, and clear.

Cord cutting meditation.

Having a terrible day at work with that one coworker, fighting with your loved ones, or feeling exhausted dealing with anyone else. Whether it's any of those listed above or something similar, This meditation technique is fantastic when you feel certain situations, people, and places draining your energy. First, be very calm and think: who or what is draining your energy? Visualize it. Whom or what exactly is it? See it right in front of you. Once you see this, visualize a blade made of crystalline white light and cut those cords. Cut all the negativity, attachment, and tension. You can repeat this meditation as much as you'd like whenever you need.

Answering your questions through meditation.

What questions have you always had in the back of your mind? What questions keep you up at night? What questions have you *always* wanted answers to? The more you meditate and clear yourself, the more accurate your messages will be. As your psychic gift expands, asking and getting answers to your questions is crucial.

In this meditation technique, you'll learn *how to* answer these questions. Seeing and hearing are the most essential parts of this technique, and that's what you'll focus on.

Firstly, get cleared. For this meditation specifically, you must make sure you are *completely* cleared. When you are entirely immersed in the light, you can start asking questions. Secondly, go still and quiet and ask to receive messages from the Divine. Be very clear when you ask to ensure you only receive messages from the Divine.

Thirdly, What do you see and hear?

Tip: Keep track of the messages you receive during your meditations.

These are a few of the many beneficial meditation techniques. The beauty is that you can experiment and even develop your signature style of meditation. Do whatever works best for you.

Pro Tip: keep a record of the meditations you've tried and what works best for you. In this record, experiment with your own.

After learning these marvelous benefits, let's learn how to implement the most important meditation technique: connecting to the Divine.

CHAPTER SIX

What is the Divine?

An existence that is beyond comprehension.

A being that transcends the laws of the physical realm and itself created them. Omniscient, knowing every detail about creation everywhere. An all-encompassing knowledge that astounds the minds of all. Omnipotent, bound to none, and eclipses all measures—a source of unlimited power, creating universes with a thought. Omnipresent, found everywhere, near and far, from beginning to end. It goes by many names, "the source," "the divine," "the creator," and "the universe," yet they all refer to the same existence, and that is *God*.

The world around us is an extraordinary symphony. With any grand melody, there is always a conductor behind it. Without this conductor, this remarkable hymn would not exist. Unlike what we are taught, this world was not created by accident. In truth, it was created intricately by the benevolent orchestrator of all, God.

Anyone can connect to the infinite spirit, one of the many benefits of tapping into your psychic gifts and intuition. Reconnecting to the divine has an *astonishing* impact on your life. Having a genuine relationship with your creator is extraordinarily soul-fulfilling. It will revolutionize your mental well-being, cultivate your awakening to higher levels of consciousness, receive marvelous guidance for your life, and open up a new level of clarity you never thought possible.

What is the Divine?

Seeing is an essential part of unlocking your psychic gifts. To see is to experience, and to experience is to step into the magic of your psychic gifts truly. A significant part of the process of unleashing your intuition is *connecting* to God. You will learn to implement this critical step later in this book. But to connect to God, you must first understand *what* God is.

Note: the divine, creator, and universe are used interchangeably to describe the true essence of life itself, God.

We've experienced that the Divine's true form is an infinitely flowing being of light. However, the Divine can also look like a body of light. The Divine is so vast that *infinity* looks like a dot compared to size. All the universes, billions of galaxies, and all the life within those galaxies all look like *a dot* compared to the Divine. But the Divine is so enormous that all life looks like a droplet in the infinite ocean of the Divine.

What shocked us the most was that our magnificent creator is *beyond* sensitive and feels everything down to its tiniest occurrence. Every single thought, feeling, action, and consequence of everything you do and everything done to you. The Divine is experiencing itself through your soul.

The one tear that you cry is felt eternally magnified by infinity. When you laugh, the Divine is in joy. When you cry, the creator is in immeasurable pain. When you breathe, the all-powerful is there, breathing with you. The Divine has experienced every single moment of your life *with* you and knows you inside and out to the deepest depths of you. Everything that you experience is felt by our creator forever.

On top of this, the Divine's love is never-ending, immeasurable, boundless, limitless, eternal, everlasting, immense, inexhaustible, unending, and immortal. It astounds us how *much* the Divine *loves* so deeply. This love is the essence of your creation and the heart of your existence in all the oceans, the vast and beautiful skies, the wondrous stars, and how the sun rises and falls.

When you laugh, the Divine is in joy. When you cry, the creator is in immeasurable pain. When you breathe, the universe is there, breathing with you. The Divine has experienced every single moment of your life *with* you and knows you inside and out to the deepest depths of you. The Divine is truly your essence.

Imagine what you love the most.

The Divine loves you like that but magnified to *infinity*, your every spec magnified into infinite, never-ending, immeasurable, boundless, limitless, eternal, everlasting, immense, inexhaustible, unending, immortal love for you. You mean so much to the Divine, more than you will ever know.

And this love is beyond fair in judgment, as free will is a gift. A gift to create beautifully, reign peace for yourself and others, and create heaven on earth. It is purely your choice. Every single day and every moment, you have a choice. A choice to spread kindness, joy, and positivity and to become a beacon of light for others. But misuse of this gift creates the opposite: pain, hatred, judgment, and becoming a carrier of darkness.

If you have a hammer, it is *your choice* to either break or fix something.

It is solely your choice what to do with it. It is *your* free will. People have free will, and it is a gift. However, many do not realize that whatever you do, it will come back to you.

You *will experience* everything you have ever done, including what you have felt, thought, said, and done to others. And be in the body of the people you have affected, experiencing everything the person felt, thought, said, and did. The laws of the universe are beyond fair, and the rule is the same for everybody. Everything you do will come back to you. This can happen in many ways. You can spread joy, and joy will come back to you. You can spread pain, and pain will find you. This doesn't have to be in the same way that you caused the pain, but that same pain you caused to others will come back to you in some way. Whether that same pain is expressed through relationships, financially, or health-wise, you will experience what you did. Why? This extraordinary world that we live in comes from a source, and that source is the Divine. Because we all come from this source, we are all connected. You are *directly connected* to all creation. You are responsible for every action you take. So choose and create wisely because your life depends on it.

CHAPTER SEVEN

Enlightenment

Congratulations. You've learned *how* to meditate. This chapter will show you some of the intuitive insights and messages we've received over the years. Receiving messages can also be known as Channeling. Channeling is a spiritual practice where you serve as a vessel for beings or energies from other realms, dimensions, or higher consciousness to communicate through you. During channeling, you allow these entities to speak or convey messages using their body, voice, or mind. It's like you temporarily set aside your consciousness to allow the external source to express itself. Channeling can take various forms, such as verbal channeling, where the channeler speaks the messages they receive, or automatic writing, where the messages are written down. Channeling provides life-changing clarity, guidance, and insight.

In our own experiences, this insight has saved us from many bad situations, led us to divinely orchestrated moments, fixed relationships in our family, relocated us to Dubai, grew our business exponentially, and ultimately, is why we wrote this book. Tapping into your psychic gifts and intuition unlocks an outpour of Divine guidance.

Messages from the Divine.

These are some of the mind-blowing messages we have received in our personal experiences with the all-mighty Divine. From eye-opening insight into the magnitude of the creator's love to illuminating the truth of how deeply connected we are to the source and creation itself to astonishing insight and guidance to benefit, help, and serve you on the journey of life, these messages are monumental to higher levels of understanding.

Section One: The Divine's Love

"I love you all so much. I have created universes and beautiful worlds that you can experience fully and truly through your form. All out of love for you, my dear creation. I have given this world to you as a gift from me. I love you infinitely, more than words can ever express. This is deeply known by your soul for an eternity. You are only remembering it now. You know everything I have taught you, as this knowledge resides in you. Life is a gift to you, my dear creation."

"I love you so fiercely that nothing can come between my love for you. I am with you for eternity. I am with you until the end of time, which there is none, as my existence and my creation goes on infinitely. I am always here. I am waiting to talk to you, and I have called out to you. Answer me, my dearest."

"I have engraved my love onto your precious heart I created—my love for you courses through your veins. My very being exists in your soul."

"I have given myself to you as a gift. Love your beautiful altar in which I live."

"I love you more than existence itself. I have created every-thing for you to experience. I love you more than any word can say; you can feel your love for me in your soul. This world is an expression of my love for you that is eternally written in your soul."

"I love you, my dear creation, with all of me; I give to all of you in different forms. The air you breathe from the trees gives you oxygen. Your heart beats to the rhythm of your soul, which is part of my intricate orchestra of design. Your body, designed as a tool for your life purpose, is given in form to you as a gift from me."

"Oh Darling Creation, don't you know how much I love you? I have loved you for an eternity, and for an eternity, I will always. My love for you surpasses *infinity*. Physically, you could say:

Faster than the speed of light,

Deeper than the vast and mighty ocean,

More powerful than the life-giving sun.

I am always there, from every breath you take to every word you say. Every thought you make to every feeling you feel, I feel with you. I am living with you, as I am your life, and you are mine.

Oh Dear Creation,

Have you forgotten what I am to you? Have you lost our communication? Do you remember what I am to you? All the magnificent moments with you and me, which I cherish for an eternity.

I live in you; I am your home. Your soul is made of me - I am your soul. At the core of your being - your very essence - you and me are one."

"I have created you to feel every bit of love from me to you. You are a divine piece of heaven on earth crafted to perfection by one who loves you the most. You may forget, but I remember everything you are to me.

You may forget what I am to *you*.

Have you forgotten everything I am to you?"

Section Two: The Divine Truth

"You are me expressed in a different form. Free will is a gift I have given to creation. It is up to you to use it wisely, as everything you do will come back to you. Nothing goes unnoticed by me, the creator of all creation, which is intricately designed. I know everything that has ever happened, happening, or will happen to you. Nothing can escape my infinite knowledge of my creation. I know more about you than you will ever know, for am I experiencing it with you? I experience all that you go through. I am living, breathing, and existing with you. When you move, I am moved. When you cry, I am crying with you. When you are happy, I am in the highest joy. When you are sad, I am in immeasurable sorrow. I exist within you; you just have to remember me. To remember that you and me are both one at the core."

"I have never forgotten you; you have just had to remember that I am here."

"Experience me, for I am your home, I am everything you have ever longed for. I am the desire that seeps into your mind, I am the yearning in your heart, and I am the calling in your soul. What you are looking for ultimately leads back to me. I am your home; come back to me. Return to me, my creation."

"The eternal truth that your soul knows for eternity is that I am you in a different form."

"I am more present than you can imagine. I am here with you all, experiencing everything you do. I am found everywhere you are and look. *I am.* I am the trees that give you oxygen and the air that fills your lungs. I am everywhere."

"Transcend this physical realm and open your eyes to everything around you. Open your heart to the truth that everything existing is a piece of me. Think of all creation as puzzle pieces to form a grander picture of me. Every single piece of this puzzle plays a part and has a purpose. Without even one of these missing, I am incomplete. You might ask why this puzzle exists. Because I exist, each of these puzzle pieces has existed from the beginning of time. The idea and concept of these puzzle pieces existed long before they appeared as pieces. In my mind, they were much needed for my completion before they came to be. Do you understand what I'm talking about? Each of your existences comes together to form a brilliant puzzle of me. There is free will, which can drastically change the original picture. You can choose to be part of a picture that creates heaven on earth or the opposite. You can choose which vision you are turning into a reality, my intended one or one that is led astray from me. It all comes down to your will and choice, as you are my much-needed counterparts. Choose me, for I have chosen you for an eternity. Together, we can change this picture."

"I am not what you think I am. You cannot put me into words, as no word truly describes my vastness or my light. I am God, yet I have many names. Your creator. The divine. The universe. But in the end, it all starts and ends with me. Do not be afraid to say my name, for I am the truth. I cannot fit into a box, for I am the one who created it. I am the light that makes up all creation. I am the one who created it. Say my name and what I truly am."

"I am boundless. I am not bound to the physical or its limitations. I have created them for you to experience. You, too, are limitless and not bound to the physical, But you must remember that first. That you are an energetic being, a soul, and at your essence, a part of me."

"What is a frequency? It's an energetic state of being. It's your true state of energy. It is essentially what you are composed of to the core. That's what a frequency is. A high frequency can create heaven on earth, my true kingdom. A low frequency can create exactly the opposite."

"Everything is energy and carries its own frequency."

Section Three: Divine Guidance

"You create from your inner state."

"As long as you consciously choose to seek me, I will always be here."

"Always remember that life is based upon your decisions. So when you create, do it mindfully. Create a world without resentment, pain, and anger. Create a world with truth, love, and harmony."

"Anyone who seeks me will find me."

"Your outer reality will always reflect your inner state."

"It all starts with you; whatever you do now will inevitably determine the future. You create the future with every action you take, every word you speak, and every thought that is home to your mind. Create mindfully and do it with intention, one that is pure and of me. One that serves a higher purpose and a grander conclusion. One that is good for yourself and the world around you and my whole creation."

"You have a choice to feel. Feel the wonder and beauty around you in each moment, or feel the sorrow and pain around you in each moment. Life is an empty canvas for you to paint, and you get to choose what colors and what the result of the picture may be. You are creating all the time, whether consciously or unconsciously. And always remember that you can change the picture anytime and create a new one. Because you are the sovereign creator of your life, you get to *choose* what to create. This is my gift to you, known as free will. You can choose whatever you want to create. You will experience what you create, so do it thoughtfully of yourself and others."

"Certain moments will pass you by like a boat floating on a river. These rocky currents will pass, so you must keep the vision of the bigger picture in your heart. Do not think of today or tomorrow, but the next moment and the future you want to create. If you fall to sorrow in this moment, it will affect the next one. I am not telling you to suppress your emotions but to feel them fully and let them go. To feel, process, and then release. Never store pent-up emotions in your heart, as they will express themselves in one way or another. Whether in a certain area of your life or your life as a whole, unexpressed emotions will always be present until released and cleared. You must find a way to healthily express these emotions without them overtaking you. Be like the moon, mastering these waves of emotions and controlling the tides of where it may take you."

Messages from the Golden Council.

The Golden Council is a group cf higher-dimensional beings that exist in the quantum realm. Their purpose is to serve humanity for the highest good, transform the vibrational frequency on earth, and uplift our consciousness to higher levels of awakening. Messages from the Golden Council are indeed legendary and truly encompass the grand awakening happening on all scales in the world right now. It is time to enlighten yourself with these messages from the Golden Council and unravel a whole new level of truth to existence and life itself.

"You are the most unique creation of the Divine."

"The golden age starts with you."

"Life is energy, frequency, and vibration. A frequency is waves of energy coming out and going out into the universe. Albert Einstein and Nikola Tesla, the most famous scientists ever, spent their lives decoding the universe. What they found is the same as what we know spiritually: that everything, life itself, is all frequency, vibration, and energy.

Every thought and feeling (and your hidden ones) go out as waves of energy into the universe, bringing you the exact match to those thoughts and feelings. Because you are a magnet of frequencies, you must always examine whatever you go through and whatever comes up. When you feel bad or something terrible is happening, you must look at it, sit and examine it. Ask for the truth of it, take that truth and take it in, and then let the rest of it go."

"Your dominant frequency is the strongest energy coming out of you. It is the exact match of whatever you are sending out. The higher your frequency is, the more peace, love, joy, miracles, abundance, and blessings you will experience. The lower your frequency is, the more pain, sadness, grief, stress, misery, and anger you will experience. Your whole life is dependent on your frequency. What I mean by this is that your inner state creates your external reality. Everything you experience comes from an energy source, and your dominant frequency creates it. Let me break it down for you so you fully understand. For example, Let's say you had your heart broken in a relationship. That pain you experienced didn't evaporate into thin air. It stayed in your energetic fields, harboring and turning that into your frequency. Frequencies change constantly depending on your feelings; however, your dominant frequency is the strongest. So, in the future, when you are trying to attract the perfect mate, this dominant frequency of pain (caused by your last relationship) is going out into the universe and is blocking your perfect relationship. Because your divine partner is carried on a frequency of love and openness from your heart, which is the exact opposite of your dominant frequency now. Instead, your heart is closed, and you fear getting hurt. Unless that pain is cleared and your dominant frequency is changed to a positive one, you will hit a brick wall every time, no matter how hard you try or what you do to attract your perfect mate. Because it isn't you or your efforts: it is your dominant frequency."

"No one chooses to get hurt. No one creates that for themselves, either. When you have a low vibration, there are many openings for low-frequency energies to get to you. This can be expressed through meeting people with low vibrations or getting into low vibrational situations. The higher your frequency is, the higher your protection is. This is why society around you tries to get your frequency as low as possible through impossible beauty standards, comparing your life to another, or constant bad news about the world. These are all efficient ways to lower your frequency. You should be aware of what is happening around you but not fall victim to it. You can change your circumstance and the world around you, and that starts by first changing within."

"Changing your frequency is not an impossible task. It is simply feeling good. It is choosing to see the beauty around you instead of the pain. It is listening to your favorite song or dancing like no one's watching. It is loving yourself unconditionally and embracing *you*. It is self-care, like taking a bath or reading a book. It is all the things that make you feel good. However, this isn't about anything external but the change you create within yourself. Your focus should not be on *doing* but rather on *feeling*. An exponential way to do this is to help others from your heart. Share your resources, put a smile on someone's face, and uplift your loved ones. It's about creating change from within, to the smallest to the biggest things."

"Many search for what they already are. Spending their whole lives looking, searching, and yearning for what already lies within. The search for love, at its core, is a desire to reconnect to the magnitude of love that created you and lies within you. To be loved is to be you because you are loved. You are loved by forces that stand with you, protect you, and care for you. You are loved by the Divine, who created you out of love. You are loved by us because we care for you magnificently. You are loved by your guardians in the spiritual realm, who watch over you perpetually. You are loved by those who have passed onto the higher realms and still stand with you today. You cannot see your cells or how they tirelessly work every moment to keep you alive, but you can feel the deep love that resides within. You can see this love in action when you tap into your psychic gifts and intuition. But truly, it is not a search for love in the physical realm. Love is a higher vibration that exists in the spiritual realm. Love cannot be found elsewhere, as it exists in higher consciousness. To love is to open your heart to the truth and let it lead you, to find yourself within, and to stop the search and look in the mirror only to find everything you've been looking for. Love is the highest vibration in all of creation. It is what makes the world go round and what keeps creation going. It is the essence of all that is."

"Imagine your life is a car. Who is driving it?

You are in the passenger seat when you are stuck in a limited state. You are a victim of circumstance; you have no power over your reality and cannot change it. When you are in the God State, the expanded higher consciousness, you are in the driver's seat.

You are in complete control of your life and where it takes you. You have the power to change your reality and create the life of miracles you were born to live. One of the main differences between these states is awareness.

A limited state is a limited awareness, limited only to the physical. It is the belief that you are a victim of circumstance; whatever life throws at you, you must deal with it. There's no way out or no way to change it. The Divine State, The Limitless Awareness, is living the absolute truth and higher consciousness. You are a part of the Divine; because of that, you have the power to create at will. It is the belief that you are in the driver's seat, limitless, in your higher consciousness and full power, and effortlessly creating and receiving miracles.

You are in control of your life, living limitlessly and creating fearlessly. Who is driving your car? Limited awareness? An old negative belief system? A low frequency? Take a step back and look at your life... Who is running it?

And if the answer is not your awakened self, and if you have realized that you are in the passenger seat, it's time to change it,

You are using the power within you. You have *so much power*—more than you could ever realize. Because you are a part of the Divine, you have the power to create. What are you creating? Whether consciously or unconsciously, you are creating all the time. Your energy goes out into your *infinite* energy fields, creating your reality. You have the power to create. Your soul is crafted magnificently by the Divine, with every detail in an intricate design.

Do you think you were created to be powerless? Or have you been *taught* that? Taught that you have *no* power, that you are a *victim*, And you shall live and die a victim of circumstance. What power do you think "circumstance" has over you? Or have you been taught that it controls your life... driving your car.

You are *so powerful*, And the *truth* is that "circumstance" has *no* power over you. *You* are driving your car, no one, and nothing else. You are the creator of your reality, and tapping into this power so you can create at will. You have been taught to suppress this power, to keep it hidden and locked away, because you are the victim of so-called..." circumstance." When you believe you are the victim of circumstance, it goes out trillions of times into your energetic fields, creating the reality that you are a victim of circumstance.

It's time you step into your power and unleash it. It's your time to be in the driver's seat.

"It always has been and always will be your car!"

Epilogue

Your Soul's Grandest Calling Yet

As the sun sets to pass, the trees lose their leaves, and the sky becomes dark; the journey comes to an end. However, is this the end? Or is it the beginning of something far greater than you've ever imagined? Because what happens when the trees are bare, the sky is filled with shadows, and the sun is seemingly nowhere in sight? Miracles are transpiring. Right around the corner, spring comes, and the trees bloom into a vibrant greatness. Swimming in its darkness, the stars that reign in the sky begin to shine their light. And the mighty sun arises like the phoenix, ascending in its radiance to light up the world once again. What may seem like the end of your journey is just the beginning of your new one.

This book was written for you. For your soul's grandest awakening yet, for you to remember the power you hold and reawaken it. For you to step into your psychic gifts and blossom wonderfully. For you to become the golden warrior that you are and *change* the world like you've always dreamed of. With all this knowledge you now have, your journey doesn't stop here; it continues into greatness. In every moment of your existence, do good, spread love, be kind, speak the truth, and create heaven on earth. It is your moment to *create* the greatest change for humanity yet. This was all divinely orchestrated for you. Now you've reached the end of this book...but as you know, the end is only the beginning. You have started your marvelous journey toward changing your life *and* the world.

With humanity in their psychic gifts and intuition, the world will change as you know it. It is heaven on earth and enlightenment for all creation. Peace on earth, harmony between all people, and no division. Where there is prosperity for everyone, humanity living in kindness and joy, and an abundance of miracles, there is infinite safety and protection for all, unity amongst families, children, and animals, and the true beauty of each soul shines through. It's time to reunite as the true golden warrior that you are and answer *your soul's grandest calling yet*. This is *your* invitation to work with us. If you are *ready* to drastically transform your life in every aspect, unleash the powers of your intuition, step into your psychic gifts, and receive your miracles, Then this is for *you*.

We are excited to receive you, as this moment has been orchestrated since the beginning of time. For an eternity, this moment has remained yearning and is now presenting itself to you. Answer the call, and we'll be waiting.

References

1. International journal of hypertension, Meditation Techniques as Treatments for Elevated Blood Pressure (March 2012)

2. American Heart Association, Meditation and Cardiovascular Risk Reduction (September 2017)

3. Mindfulness meditation and the immune system: a systematic review of Randomized controlled trials (January 2016)

Contact

SOCIAL MEDIA PROFILES

@yamunahasan

instagram.com/yamunahasan/

@ayeshahasanofficial

instagram.com/ayeshahasanofficial/

@godsmiraclesforyou

instagram.com/godsmiraclesforyou/

linkedin.com/in/gods-miracles-for-you-57863247/